BOOKS BY WILLIAM MEREDITH

THE OPEN SEA AND OTHER POEMS

THE OPEN SEA

AND OTHER POEMS BY

WILLIAM MEREDITH

NEW YORK  *ALFRED A. KNOPF 1958*

811

ACKNOWLEDGMENTS: The earliest poems in this collection were written during the tenure of a fellowship from the Rockefeller Foundation granted for a study of obscurity in modern poetry. The latest poems were written while I held a Hudson Review Fellowship in poetry. Acknowledgment is made to the editors of the following publications where some of these poems first appeared: The Hudson Review, The Ladies Home Journal, New Poets of England and America (Meridian Books), Partisan Review, Poetry, The Saturday Review, The Sewanee Review, The Virginia Quarterly Review, and The New Yorker, where the following poems originally appeared: *Battle Problem, Thoughts on One's Head, Godchildren, Ablutions,* and *On Falling Asleep by Firelight.*

L. C. catalog card number: 58–5824

© *William Meredith,* 1957

This is a BORZOI BOOK, published by ALFRED A. KNOPF, INC.

FIRST EDITION

IN MEMORY OF DONALD A. STAUFFER

Armed with an indiscriminate delight
His ghost left Oxford five summers ago,
Still on the sweet, obvious side of right.

How many friends and students talked all night
With this remarkable teacher? How many go
Still armed with his indiscriminate delight?

He liked, but often could not reach, the bright:
Young people sometimes prefer not to know
About the sweet or obvious sides of right.

But how all arrogance involves a slight
To knowledge, his humility would show
Them, and his indiscriminate delight

In what was true. This was why he could write
Commonplace books: his patience lingered so
Fondly on the sweet, obvious side of right.

What rare anthology of ghosts sits till first light
In the understanding air where he talks now,
Armed with his indiscriminate delight
There on the sweet and obvious side of right?

THE OPEN SEA AND OTHER POEMS

The Open Sea

We say the sea is lonely; better say
Ourselves are lonesome creatures whom the sea
Gives neither yes nor no for company.

Oh, there are people, all right, settled in the sea—
It is as populous as Maine today—
But no one who will give you the time of day.

A man who asks there of his family
Or a friend or teacher gets a cold reply
Or finds him dead against that vast majority.

Nor does it signify that people who stay
Very long, bereaved or not, at the edge of the sea
Hear the drowned folk call: that is mere fancy,

They are speechless. And the famous noise of sea,
Which a poet has beautifully told us in our day,
Is hardly a sound to speak comfort to the lonely.

Although not yet a man given to prayer, I pray
For each creature lost since the start at sea,
And give thanks it was not I, nor yet one close to me.

Sonnet on Rare Animals

Like deer rat-tat before we reach the clearing
I frighten what I brought you out to see,
Telling you who are tired by now of hearing
How there are five, how they take no fright of me.
I tried to point out fins inside the reef
Where the coral reef had turned the water dark;
The bathers kept the beach in half-belief
But would not swim and could not see the shark.
I have alarmed on your behalf and others'
Sauntering things galore.
It is this way with verse and an'mals
And love, that when you point you lose them all.
Startled or on a signal, what is rare
Is off before you have it anywhere.

Notre Dame de Chartres

After God's house burned down, they found the shirt—
His mother Mary's shirt; it had not burned.
This was their kind of miracle: it spoke
Of continuing grace, if chastised. The Lord's mother
Would stay on; it was simply that the house
Had not pleased the holy visitor to France.

The town's good fortune must have stirred all France,
The preservation of that sacred shirt
Which had won battles for the royal house;
The citizens themselves whose town had burned
To the ground that night, thanked God's gracious mother
For the special favor that the flames bespoke.

The vast basilica they raised there spoke
Of a yearning that reached far beyond France,
A love that verged on heresy for the mother
Who had been brought to bed in this same shirt.
This is our miracle: the faith that burned
Bright and erroneous, and built that house.

I suppose there never will be such a house
Again, that has the power to make men speak
Of *an act of God*, where a dozen cities burned
Will not; to ask a pilgrimage to France
Of men and women who smile about the shirt
And doubt or know nothing of the mother.

The arbitrary doctrine of the Mother
Is no harder to believe than her great house
At Chartres, copied from heaven, to hold a shirt.
Stand at the transept when the delicate spokes
Of stone glow black against the sun of France:
It is as if the virgin's faith still burned.

Or as if the ancient glass itself still burned,
If you prefer that to the legend of God's mother.
Whatever it is, no splendor now in France
Puzzles the heart like the molten light in this house;
Probably no one who saw it ever spoke
Coarsely again of the medieval shirt.

Sancta Camisa, the blessed shirt of the Mother,
Because it had not burned, required a house
And spoke to the stone that slept in the groin of France.

Starlight

Going abruptly into a starry night
It is ignorance we blink from, dark, unhoused;
There is a gaze of animal delight
Before the human vision. Then, aroused
To nebulous danger, we may look for easy stars,
Orion and the Dipper; but they are not ours,

These learned fields. Dark and ignorant,
Unable to see here what our forebears saw,
We keep some fear of random firmament
Vestigial in us. And we think, Ah,
If I had lived then, when these stories were made up, I
Could have found more likely pictures in haphazard sky.

But this is not so. Indeed, we have proved fools
When it comes to myths and images. A few
Old bestiaries, pantheons and tools
Translated to the heavens years ago—
Scales and hunter, goat and horologe—are all
That save us when, time and again, our systems fall.

And what would we do, given a fresh sky
And our dearth of image? Our fears, our few beliefs
Do not have shapes. They are like that astral way
We have called milky, vague stars and star-reefs
That were shapeless even to the fecund eye of myth—
Surely these are no forms to start a zodiac with.

To keep the sky free of luxurious shapes
Is an occupation for most of us, the mind
Free of luxurious thoughts. If we choose to escape,
What venial constellations will unwind
Around a point of light, and then cannot be found
Another night or by another man or from other ground.

As for me, I would find faces there,
Or perhaps one face I have long taken for guide;
Far-fetched, maybe, like Cygnus, but as fair,
And a constellation anyone could read
Once it was pointed out; an enlightenment of night,
The way the pronoun *you* will turn dark verses bright.

On Falling Asleep by Firelight

The wolf and the lamb shall feed together, and the lion shall eat straw like the bullock, and dust shall be the serpent's meat. ISAIAH 65

Around the fireplace, pointing at the fire,
As in the prophet's dream of the last truce,
The animals lie down; they doze or stare,
Their hooves and paws in comical disuse;
A few still run in dreams. None seems aware
Of the laws of prey that lie asleep here too,
The dreamer unafraid who keeps the zoo.

Some winter nights impel us to take in
Whatever lopes outside, beastly or kind;
Nothing that gibbers in or out of mind
But the hearth bestows a sleepy sense of kin.
Promiscuous hosts, we bid the causeless slime
Come in; its casualness remains a crime
But metaphysics bites less sharp than wind.

Now too a ghostly, gradually erect
Company lies down, weary of the walk,
Parents with whom we would but cannot talk;
Beside them on the floor, their artifacts—
Weapons we gave them which they now bring back.
If they see our privilege, they do not object,
And we are not ashamed to be their stock.

All we had thought unkind were all the while
Alike, the firelight says and strikes us dumb;
We dream there is no ravening or guile
And take it kindly of the beasts to come
And suffer hospitality; the heat
Turns softly on the hearth into that dust
Isaiah said would be the serpent's meat.

The Illiterate

Touching your goodness, I am like a man
Who turns a letter over in his hand
And you might think this was because the hand
Was unfamiliar but, truth is, the man
Has never had a letter from anyone;
And now he is both afraid of what it means
And ashamed because he has no other means
To find out what it says than to ask someone.

His uncle could have left the farm to him,
Or his parents died before he sent them word,
Or the dark girl changed and want him for beloved.
Afraid and letter-proud, he keeps it with him.
What would you call his feeling for the words
That keep him rich and orphaned and beloved?

From *Ritual to Romance*

We are saved by love the way the fisherman
In the myth is cured by the knowledgeable knight
Who, step by step and counter to the ban,
Works a unique and superstitious rite
That frees the waters, and suddenly they run
Through the fisher-king's domain, the silver blight
Quits his wheat, and his dry herds begin
To calve, and the king himself to govern right.

This is the way throughout the sick estate
Where love effects its ruthless cure of will;
The will restored restores the whole to health.
Finish the working of your arcane rite,
Stay with me just this lifetime or until
No one can maim me, even I myself.

A*blutions*

Sweet influences keep the planet sweet
Of what the beasts make bitter:
Shores by the tides, the fields by rain delete
Our bodies and bodies' litter

While the heavy exhalation that the flesh
Gives off in burning
Is laved in a thinner effluence kept fresh
By the planet's always turning.

Sunrise with Crows

Seeing the sun rise will not mend this day.
I went out in dark among crows older than I am,
By the sound of them, forgetting their summer-counts
But destined to see sixty; and when the sun came up
Red and straight—that always ambiguous omen—
These crows who had never missed a sunrise
Were badly-adjusted; at sunrise these crows,
Neither attracted nor repelled, were vaguely cawing.
Then I heard the vehicles shifting of a world
As sad and various as the reasons that I've seen,
All told, perhaps some fifty perfect dawns.
Now I can not think what to tell the sleeping
Against whom I had taken this walk,
The optimists I love, who will never settle
For a negative account of the famous miracle—
A gold sunrise flecked with crows—
Hailed as a mend-all in China, in Greece,
In a dozen fragile citadels that lie
Shattered to fragments no bigger than a man.

A *View of the Brooklyn Bridge*

The growing need to be moving around it to see it,
To prevent its freezing, as with sculpture and metaphor,
Finds now skeins, now strokes of the sun in a dark
Crucifixion etching, until you end by caring
What the man's name was who made it,
The way old people care about names and are
Forever seeing resemblances to people now dead.

Of stone and two metals drawn out so
That at every time of day
They speak out of strong resemblances, as:
Wings whirring so that you see only where
Their strokes finish, or: spokes of dissynchronous wheels.

Whose pictures and poems could accurately be signed
With the engineer's name, whatever he meant,
And be called: *Tines inflicting a river, justly*,
Or (thinking how its cables owe each something
To the horizontal and something to the vertical):
A graph of the odds against
Any one man's producing a masterpiece.

Yet far from his, the engineer's, at sunrise
And again at sunset when,
Like the likenesses the old see,
Loveliness besets it as haphazard as genes:
Fortunate accidents take the form of cities
At either end; the cities give their poor edges
To the river, the buildings there
The fair color that things have to be.
Oh the paper reeds by a brook
Or the lakes that lie on bayous like a leopard
Are not at more seeming random, or more certain
In their sheen how to stand, than these towns are.

And of the rivering vessels so and so
Where the shadow of the bridge rakes them once,
The best you can think is that, come there,
A pilot will know what he's done
When his ship is fingered

Like that Greek boy whose name I now forget
Whose youth was one long study to cut stone;
One day his mallet slipped, some goddess willing
Who only meant to take his afternoon,
So that the marble opened on a girl
Seated at music and wonderfully fleshed
And sinewed under linen, riffling a harp;
At which he knew not that delight alone
The impatient muse intended, but, coupled with it, grief—
The harp-strings in particular were so light—
And put his chisel down for marvelling on that stone.

Godchildren

Children of mine, not mine but lent
By generous parents, what sweet grief
I take from our clumsy make-belief,
Neither fulfilled nor discontent.

From my mock-parenthood I learn
Domestic uses, while you feed
Promiscuously in your need
For love, and all love serves your turn.

The bond I gave to set you free
In childhood was my soul in prayer.
I had not thought to bargain there
But you stand sponsors now for me.

My fantasy is this: alone,
Like orphans in reverse, are whirled
The seedless god-folk of the world
And then redeemed by this bright loan.

Waterways

On favorable terms I have somehow been
Diminished imperceptibly, like an island city
Where the streets, each with its own excuse,
Take half the land at last and give no thoroughfare.
Now a commission views it from the air,
Too late by years to lay out parks and traffic
On anything like the scale the site suggests.

But wherever I strike the waterfront, on my walks,
Moves evenly one of two gull-soared rivers;
It boils with the salt tide and its headwaters;
It is at the full with early water, changing the banks.
And here the city, all port, gives on the ocean generously
Like a man who, if with regard to love only,
Is determined he will not take terms.

An Account of a Visit to Hawaii

Snow through the fronds, fire flowing into the sea
At a goddess' will who does not ask belief—
It is hard to reconcile extremities
Of any size, or to find their centers out,
As paradoxes demonstrate, and griefs,
And this old kingdom running sweetly out.
You would not think to say of a custom here
'This is the place itself,' as you might elsewhere.

There are no snakes and very little lust;
Many decorums have made life decorous.
Fish stands for food and hospitality,
And the innocence of symbols generally
Is surprising, now that we think absurd
The Noble Savage. *Mildmercy*—one word—
Is perhaps the closest European concept
To name the culture, surely to name the climate

Which has the ocean's powers of deception
When unrippled. The women stringing flowers
To keep the shade describe a slow ellipse
From June to June, like sun-dials at their hours.
And people have mistaken toy ships
For the ship to take them back across the ocean
And later stayed too long. The practical
Chinese put ripples in the year with catherine wheels.

Mildness can enervate as well as heat.
The soul must labor to reach paradise.
Many are here detained in partial grace
Or partial penalty, for want of force.
The canefields burn in fire that does no harm,
The cataracts blow upward in the Trades,
For all the world as if there were no rules.
It is no easy place to save the soul.

And there is danger to the native pride
Of a land where dreams make the economy.
Like tourists, dreams distort the things they buy
And float an easy currency, until
There is no talking to the native heart.
Nightly descending through the baroque cloud
That decorates these hills, riding on air,
Thousands arrive by dream at their desire.

One of the last kings sold the Sandlewood
To buy a fleet. For every ship, they filled
An excavation dug to match the hull.
You can see these to this day—volcanic soil
Falls chunk by chunk into the phantom holds.
It rains at night. The trees the old king sold
Do not grow back. The islands have their perils
Which if you do not feel, no one can tell you.

This is another meaning for *aloha*,
A greeting as ambiguous as the place:
Not a promiscuous welcome to all strangers,
But what is more hospitable than that,
Warning of taboos and a hundred dangers—
Whether to you, you must decide alone.
And if it is not safe to come here yet,
One of the things *aloha* means is: wait.

A place to live when you are reconciled
To beauty and unafraid of time.
(They languish, abstract, when no more opposed.)
A place to earn in more chastising climates
Which teach us that our destinies are mild
Rather than fierce as we had once supposed,
And how to recognize the peril of calm,
Menaced only by surf and flowers and palms.

M*iniature*

One of the gentlest, as it looks from here,
Of Persian ways is how the shy are known
And looked on in the matter of their needs—
The shy, the disparate, the merely odd.
I have not been to Persia but they tell
How nothing is too much trouble all at once
For irritable beaters when a shy man hunts.
A forest bird was heard to trill for two,
Awkward in one another's presence still—
Two ornithologists—over and over until
They had noted down its call in turquoise curls
On the scrolls they paint with pictures of the fowl.
In the spiced equivalents of cafés there
Waiters grow civil to the ill-matched pair,
The bald and raven-haired, the strong and halt;
And indeed everyone is delicate
Of their delays, of just that complication
That makes at last their loves incapable.
While in the Persian darkness clop clop clop
What is perhaps most courteous of all,
The bold and coarse ride off time and again
To do what must be done in violence.

The Fishvendor

Where he stood in boots in water to his calves,
A kind of fisherman, dispensing with a dip-net
Sullen carp into the tubs of ice,
Was only in a tank on the back of a truck.
Blocks off, gulls rung and fell to investigate
What they took to be sardine cans
On the river shiningly; but who contended
For his thick brown fish were rather wives
With boiling dishes in their eyes,
Women estranged by city from live water;
Where even the cats did not wait for the heads,
The scene was that strong.

While the mistaken sea-birds thrust the city away
With a salt vigor,
I heard the fisherman's feet shift in the brine,
The thick fish thrashing without resignation,
The shoppers, half tame at noon,
Naming the coins that routed all of the cats
And were for salt and instinct to a city.

Original *Aversions*

In all respects unready for a fall
They fell, our first progenitors, and these
Two traumas still disturb us most of all:
High places and our own unreadiness.
Towers or wells unfoot us in our dreams
Repeatedly. Old-fashioned people still
Believe that nothing saves them but their screams
And that an unawakened fall would kill.
Anticipation cannot really ease
The other trouble; waiting for the day
When such and such will happen or will pass,
It is not hard to wish your life away.
Apart from angels, wingèd and prevised,
Nobody likes to fall or be surprised.

To *Absent Friends*

It may be no one is absent who is thought of.
This wordy game—the Bishop and the Quad—
Beguiles departed lovers, who may be said
With a certain accuracy to exist through love.
But how we others are gathered under the sky,
Welkin-friends, ruined or happy, alive or dead,
Doing each other favors, praising God,
Is in a droller, much less verbal way.

Like Irishmen, we only think the best
Of people, once inside the smoky bar
Of our regard. The firelight makes them tall,
As close to heroes and heroines as yeast
Will leaven fact. And though we drink no more
Together, those grave and blarney roles we cast
Each other in years since stick with us still,
And friend acts out friend's hero to the last.

The Fear of Beasts

Pity the nightly tiger: fierce and wise,
He works upwind; the moonlight stripes his glade;
No one could hear that tread,
Least of all his guileless, watering prize.
And yet, the wonder is, he is afraid.
At the water-hole, one look from dreaming eyes,
From sleeping throat the feeblest of cries,
Will prove ambush enough to strike him dead.
A beast in a human dream must go in dread
Of the chance awakening on which he dies.

The Chinese Banyan

There is no end to the
Deception of quiet things
And of quiet, everyday
People a lifetime brings.
Take a kind of Banyan tree
That grows in the temperate islands
Where a friend lived recently:
With what commendable violence
The shallow roots—as blunt
As earthworms in the dark,
As blunt and as unremarked—
Make for what they want.
At night on their way to drink
They will rend like little dooms
(The last thing you would think)
Impediments of stone;
The last thing in the world
You would think of, seeing the crown
Of pale leaves just unfurled
That the breeze moves up and down.

And the friend himself who stayed
In the islands, his small roof
Taking a Banyan's shade—
That life was quiet enough:
Teacher and bachelor,
Hard forces both to measure.
With Sammy, a small white cur,
Who would dance or yap for pleasure,

He lived in the four-room house
Under the small-leafed tree
Where counter to his wish
We said an obsequy.
The water had run in the sink
All night, for his heart had burst
While he drew the dog a drink;
And what he muttered first
Only Sammy the dog knew
Who stayed in the kitchen till dawn
As dogs have agreed to do.
A quiet, temperate man:
We have all known dearer loss.
But I speak of the unremarked
Forces that split the heart
And make the pavement toss—
Forces concealed in quiet
People and plants, until
At some silent blood riot
Or sap riot, they spill;
And this dark capacity
Of quiet looses a fear
That runs by analogy
On your page, in your house, for your dear.

The Rainy Season

As boring as the fact of a marvelous friend
Told at some length by strangers while you nod
From the booth of yourself and wait your turn
Are these rains that detain these nights

                         Until you think
What they say on each roof, awake in its own dismay:
Like the reproof of that singular good man,
Unknown to you, to whom you are unknown,
Told at some length by strangers while you nod;
And not unlike the signs in rainy bars
That read themselves at the poor edge of sleep:
The lie too complicated to refute:
If you're so damn smart, why aren't you rich?

To a Western Bard still a Whoop and a Holler away from English Poetry

I read an impatient man
Who howls against his time,
Not angry enough to scan
Not fond enough to rhyme,

And I think of the terrible cry
The brave priest Hopkins raised
The night he raided the sky
And English verse was praised.

And the infinite, careful woe
That informs the song of Blake,
The stricter because he knew
The jog that madmen take.

Or our own great poet's rage,
Yeats', in his decorous care
To make singing of old age
And numbers of despair.

It is common enough to grieve
And praise is all around;
If any cry means to live
It must be an uncommon sound.

Cupped with the hands of skill
How loud their voices ring,
Containing passion still,
Who cared enough to sing.

The Alchemist
(A PUBLIC READING)

In terms of years—
Old man, great heart—
He has few peers
And none in terms of art:
Laughter and tears
Can set a man apart.

He puts a spell
Of runic stories
Over the summer hall;
And if he wearies
A little, after all,
Of poems and theories

Remember: apart and old
Is a great cost,
And nothing has been sold
Here, nothing lost—
He still makes gold:
The poems of Robert Frost.

In Memoriam N.K.M. (1889–1947)

As the day takes color twice, so youth and age
Should glow remarkably. Or, like a maple's
I wish her fall had been (whose quaint April
Is still in blossom on the album's pages)
Splendid and red, which was a sere, gray loss.
Like a round maple, if that could just have been,
Whose virtuous green summer went unseen
In a mild chemistry, but at first frost
Who stuck across herself and her slight hill
Patterns no elm would dream of, crooked and true
Like the serene old trees on a chinese scroll:
This is a thing I have seen maples do.
The sun and trees glowed fiercely at the season
When she wandered listless forth bereft of reason.

The Fear of Death Disturbs Me

Now it is almost certain that we will be going.
The place is thought to be foul, whether defiled
By ourselves (who are variously seen as knowing
Or unknowing offenders) or befouled
Like a public lavatory by no one knows whom—
The mucker we all agree about, whose nick-name
Is all he ever scrawls in the filthy room.
But whoever the vandal is, it is all the same:

We will have to quit the ambient sweet air
For dankness and stench where, mustered one by one
By bullies, some of us they say will give
A poor account, a worse even than here.
With this much notice something should be done,
Yet what is there to do but try to live?

Bachelor

A mystic in the morning, half asleep,
He is given a vision of the unity
That informs a small apartment, barefooted.
He takes the long view of toes in the bath-tub
And shaves a man whose destiny is mild.
He perceives hidden resemblances; particularly
He is struck by how breakfast equipment imitates her,
The object of his less than mystic dream.
Sunlight, orange-juice, newsprint, kitchenware:
Is it love's trick of doubling? Everywhere
Like those little dogs in Goya, objects show
A gift for mimicry. His coffee is morose.
A clock goes off next-door where probably
Someone has parodied his dream; and here
The solemn little mongrels of the day
Stare out at him, trying to look like her.
They leer and flirt.
                    Let saints and painters deal
With the mystery of likeness. As for him,
It scares him wide awake and dead alone;
A man of action dials the telephone.

Homage to a Rake-Hell

Few people are qualified to grow old   LA ROCHEFOUCAULD

When time had got his hair and made him well-
Behaved at last, as clearly nothing else
Could do, he had the spirit not to tell
What little he had learned in erring, false.
Wracked by his prostate as he should have been
Decades before by conscience or at least,
For heaven's sake, by taste, he could retain
This honor: he did not repent his waste.
Although his cronies had grown, *faute de mieux*, wise,
He would make no virtue of incapacity.
With equal scorn for temperance and lies
He recalled his meals and veneries accurately.
An unseemly old man, surely; and yet he knew
Honor of a sort, and not all old men do.

Two *Japanese Poems*

PICTURE OF A CASTLE

Now I am tired of being Japanese
The Daimyo said, after a certain war.
Let there be a kempt jungle in a valley
And from it rise
So that you look through horizontal blossoms
A tall, unmoated fortress where the dolphins
On the gables, tails in the sky,
Swim from the separate quarters of the kingdom
Without thinking;
And with a balcony to every hour
Facing the hills, apart,
Where a sweet particular girl will say the truth
Over and over until I take it in.

AT THE KABUKI-ZA

This lady wobbles down the flowerway
To show: one, she is leisurely and gay,
And two, the play of all that gold brocade
Over the human form (there is a maid
To hold the weight up of her two gold sleeves),
And three, what no one really quite believes
Anymore, that she is a puppet anyway.

35

Two Korean Poems

FULL CIRCLE

The farmer in the round hat
Who treads the waterwheel
In the dust of the jeep road
At the turn of summer,
Wants a philosophy
Older than wheels.

OLD ONES

The old woman and the old man
Who came a day's journey to see the airfield,
Having nothing to keep them at home,
Slide down the embankment of rubble
Like frisky children
Under the starboard wing as we taxi by.
They are afraid of the roar. Also they know
Better than we that anything can happen.

Pastoral

The girl lies down on the hill
In the grass in the sun in June.
Love calls for the breaking of will;
The young man knows that soon

His will to be free must break,
And his ego, dear as a wife;
His hand is a brown mistake
Lacing him into life.

As blank as a flower, her face
Is full of the meadow's musk
And the shadow of grass like lace
On the hill where she wills the dusk.

Thoughts on One's Head (IN PLASTER, WITH A BRONZE WASH)

A person is very self-conscious about his head.
It makes one nervous just to know it is cast
In enduring materials, and that when the real one is dead
The cast one, if nobody drops it or melts it down, will last.

We pay more attention to the front end, where the face is,
Than to the interesting and involute interior:
The Fissure of Rolando and such queer places
Are parks for the passions and fears and mild hysteria.

The things that go on there! Erotic movies are shown
To anyone not accompanied by an adult.
The marquee out front maintains a superior tone:
Documentaries on Sharks and The Japanese Tea Cult.

The fronts of some heads are extravagantly pretty.
These are the females. Men sometimes blow their tops
About them, launch triremes, sack a whole city.
The female head is mounted on rococo props.

Judgment is in the head somewhere; it keeps sums
Of pleasure and pain and gives belated warning;
This is the first place everybody comes
With bills, complaints, writs, summons, in the morning.

This particular head, to my certain knowledge
Has been taught to read and write, make love and money,
Operate cars and airplanes, teach in a college,
And tell involved jokes, some few extremely funny.

It was further taught to know and to eschew
Error and sin, which it does erratically.
This is the place the soul calls home just now.
One dislikes it of course: it is the seat of Me.

*L*etter from Mexico (VERA CRUZ, 10 FEBRUARY, 186–)

You entrusted the boy to me. He has died
Along with his comrades, poor young soul. The crew—
There is no more crew; and whether the last few
Of us see France again, fate will decide.

No role a man can choose becomes him more
Than the sailor's. Perhaps it is for this
That landsmen resent him: that they do is sure.
Think what a hard apprenticeship it is.

I weep to write this, I, old Leather-Face.
Death is indifferent to what hide he tans;
Would God he'd taken mine in the lad's place.
Yet this was not my fault nor any man's;

The fever strikes like clock-work; someone falls
Each hour. The cemetery sets a ration—
Which place my sergeant (a Parisian) calls,
After his zoo, *le jardin d'acclimatation.*

Console yourself. Life crushes men like flies.
—In his sea-bag were these trophies: a girl's face,
Two little slippers, probably the size
'For his sister,' as the note inside one says.

He sent his mother word: that he had prayed;
His father: that he would have liked some bolder
Death, in battle. At the last two angels stayed
Beside him there. A sailor. An old soldier.

TRANSLATED FROM TRISTAN CORBIÈRE

A *Little Tour of the British Isles*

By Dingle Bay in Ireland,
Beyond the English Pale,
We languished for a window
In the high Palladian jail.
The water lapping Ireland
Repeated tales of wrong
But we heard the venial turn-key
Whistling our song.

The Firth of Tay was talking
The day we hit Dundee
Of nothing but our wedding
And how happy we would be.
From Blairgowrie to Leven
The gentry beat their gongs
While Calvinists told rosaries
And Trappists sang our songs.

We have settled down in London
Where the Thames is undone
And romance sits unbuttoned
In the weak winter sun.
Was it all too propitious?
Where we stroll the banks along
The old swans that flow by
Are singing our song.

A *Botanical Trope*

Regret, a bright meander on the nights
Of the driver coming always to the turn
Where the child was killed, regret is a design
As repetitious as the dogwood's veined
Descent, in autumn, from the twig to root.

At night, for all the world as if it mattered,
The bankrupt tries to fix his first mistake;
His thoughts concenter there monotonously,
As the commerce of the dogwood centers where
It borrows blossoms: at the rich black bole.

And all night long the embezzler reviews
The diagram of greed that pulled him under.
How could he hope to see, involved like that,
That his was not unlike the dogwood's scheme
To pay back all its foliage in the spring.

Unwittingly a tossing man will draw
The family of his guilt as a thick tree.
That is the winter time. The sap goes down
In grave, unhoping penance to the root,
And neither tree nor man knows to what end.

The ruined nights of men are no less praise
Than slopes of dogwood on a winter day,
Suggesting springtime only to the blind
Or sentimental—trees of the cross, some say—
Soughing together in divine remorse.

Questions for a Sculptor

Climbing the library stair where the morning sun
Tunnels in the motes, I met Margaret's face
This morning, running. There is another chin

Here like hers, her blunt nose and her eyes
Exactly, faraway Margaret an ocean ago,
A leafing and unleafing from this place.

But in this face, sun-circled by the glow
Of the white wall below on Margaret's hair
(Which is as soft as air, amber or yellow)

And in those eyes that fell at my long stare
As Margaret's might have done, lacking her pride,
Someone else was in possession there.

The work of beauty is all done inside
And never twice the same: I could not know
What had gone on behind the face I tried

To turn to Margaret's. And all beauty grows
In trouble, which again we only guess
At. Running in sunshine, I could only know
There are two ways to make a single face.

*   *   *

Hills that are like his own nobody minds:
Beauty of place is strangely of a kind.
But not the most sentimental traveller finds
Pleasure in chins or noses that remind.

*   *   *

Which brings me to the questions I would put.
Are there in fact fine points and little lines
Between the features, and we read from them
Records of work and love we cannot see,
Like Margaret's? The way that, at removes
Greater than we could hear a little cry,
We weigh the white against the white of eye
And tell that we are seen, particularly
In questions of detection or of love?

And why, as a child, when I saw a man whose gait
Was like my father's once come down our street
Out of the evening sun and railroad train,
Slapping his trouser as my father did
With his newspaper, and I ran to the man,
Was he deformed? Although complete and sound,
And thumped by my taller father for a friend,
That neighbor stays a cripple in my sleep
For differing so slightly in the shoulders.

And I will ask you at another time
About the dead friend that I see in crowds
Whose ship was lost, and now whose head I find
Is bigger than I knew it (from behind,
The way I always see him). Will this be
My faulty recollection, or the sea,
Or the grotesqueness of similarity?

Three Occasional Poems

ON TRAVELLING LIGHT
(*A little Prothalamion for a lady flying to her wedding*)

Love is a place of alchemy. Once there
You will find gold copies of everything you own.
With only the light accoutrements of air
Love should be flown to as soon as he is known.

PATRIOTIC VERSE FOR MAY

Today some twenty dogwood opened wide
Their ivory bracts; we say the hill's a bride
Which local maps still call Mount Bloody-Red
After the May when twenty Tories bled.
For this we should mistrust the eyes that see
One hill at a time, and not hyperbole.

A CHRISTMAS RUNE

The rune-delighting Maker,
Feasting the time of year
That goes against His nature,
Blossomed in the frore;

Or so it seems to His reason-
Loving creature, who will ponder
Theories of every foison
But not relax and wonder.

A Korean Woman Seated by a Wall

Suffering has settled like a sly disguise
On her cheerful old face. If she dreams beyond
Rice and a roof, now toward the end of winter,
Is it of four sons gone, the cries she has heard,
A square farm in the south, soured by tents?
Some alien and untranslatable loss
Is a mask she smiles through at the weak sun
That is moving north to invade the city again.

A poet penetrates a dark disguise
After his own conception, little or large.
Crossing the scaleless asia of trouble
Where it seems no one could give himself away,
He gives himself away, he sets a scale.
Hunger and pain and death, the sorts of loss,
Dispute our comforts like peninsulas
Of no particular value, places to fight.
And what it is in suffering dismays us more:
The capriciousness with which it is dispensed
Or the unflinching way we see it borne?

She may be dreaming of her wedding gift;
A celadon bowl of a good dynasty
With cloud and heron cut in its green paste,
It sleeps in a hollow bed of pale blue silk.
The rice it bought was eaten the second winter.
And by what happier stove is it unwrapped
In the evening now and passed around like a meat,
Making a foliage in the firelight?

46

She shifts the crate she sits on as the March
Wind mounts from the sea. The sun moves down the sky
Perceptibly, like the hand of a public clock,
In increments of darkness though ablaze.
Ah, now she looks at me. We are unmasked
And exchange what roles we guess at for an instant.
The questions Who comes next and Why not me
Rage at and founder my philosophy.
Guilt beyond my error and a grace past her grief
Alter the coins I tender cowardly,
Shiver the porcelain fable to green shards.

Battle Problem

A company of vessels on the sea
Running in darkness, like a company
Of stars or touchless martyrs in the fields
Above, or a wan school beneath its keels,
Holds a discrete deployment.

                        Men who ride
In the ships are borne by no calculable tide:
Hurtled untouched, untouching, side by side
They sit at table, sleep in beds, keep shops
In marvelous spirals that reconcile the ship's
Way and the world's, the spinning and ellipse.
They hardly feel the weather; they do not feel
The ships around them or the planets wheel.
Trusting the several forces that direct
Things parallel, they will not intersect.

Moved by safe appetites, like the older stars,
The saints, and certain migratory creatures,
Older men conn the darkened ships at sea
In not the usual sense of company.

R*us in Urbe*

In a city garden an espaliered tree
Like Shiva, handling the brick south wall,
Or better, like a Jesse Tree, holds big
Real pears on each contrived square bough.
And in a tub, a yew turned like a top,
Which might as easily have been a peacock
Or half of a deer, in the unnatural kingdom
Of topiary, where the will is done,
Is lovely to the point you would not ask
What would have been its genius, uncut?
Any more than: what did the rock look like
Before Praxiteles cut it away?
Then this whole garden four flights toward the sun
Raised by no tropism, but its uselessness
In a strict place, the humus carried there
In wooden trays. The vegetation thrives;
The laws hold; and there may be a rich woman
Saved somehow in the evening by the green.

The Deciduous Trees

A tree is no more leaves than a person days:
Take color, take fire, take flight,
Shut of the clutter of leaves,
You see what tensions are rife
All year inside the trees,
All built, like bridges, of stress.

Autumned at heart, where no man is evergreen,
The gaunt reach of a man
Is, if not stress only, yet known
Once for himself, at least once seen.
And before a filament of green
Makes seemly cover to that discovery,
There is all winter to clack through:
Twigs in the gale, splayed to a gray sky,
The shape of a man springs up,
A wraith at a field's corner
To the swaddled passer-by.

In *A Time of Blight*

The beeches have come to harm
Which were the poet's tree
And once down the farthest arm
Of Maine and lean Acadie
Reached to the bitter sea;
Like the pigeon whose fare
They were, the beeches grow rare,
Hewn from the forest fence
First for their excellence.
A tree in a grove seems my love to me.

As if man were in new disgrace
Elms lose their leaves in June.
Trees that keep sky in place,
Scaling the huge light
Of forenoon and, afternoon,
The thunderheads' bloom;
Trees that like fountains spring
Now feel a cureless blight.
I fear for all tall things.
A tree in a grove seems my love to me.

Trees in a Grove

Of five things put in mind by sycamores,
I think first of a sad baldheaded man
In a pepper-and-salt tweed suit who knew the trees
And pointing them out on tree-walks in our suburb
Would tell their myths and virtues with their names,
The sovereign words by which a child takes hold.

I was seven the summer that I first got hold
Of the white pied spicy word of sycamore,
The age when children will incant new names.
That night I dreamt I was a flying man
And could escape the backyard of our suburb
By saying sycamore, rise through the trees.

Abroad and serious, I found the trees
That over Hopkins' towery city hold
A hill unspoiled by view of its brick suburbs.
Jump at the crown a transposed sycamore
Did what a simple thing will, made men
For me of Hopkins, Arnold, Glanvil, once just names.

Fourth, I am summoned at the white tree's name
To where I held love at the foot of forest trees.
I wondered what on earth could happen to a man
Once he had had such a precious thing to hold,
Had known successful love under a sycamore
Huge and tameless as though there were no suburbs.

As old houses stand exemplary in suburbs
With scanty grounds, lending their proud names
To rows of tenements, so two sycamores
King and queen it in my mind's trees:
They are lean candelabra and now they hold
Hard flambeaux for a willow-thinking man;

And now they are sea-images to a dry landsman
Who would not willingly quit his sitfast suburb
But seeing the watery pearl fingers hold
To the March clouds like drogues, he calls their name,
And is changed to a seaman naming coral trees
Where they fret exotic seas like sycamores.

And it is prudent sycamores should hold
Our thoughts: suburbs eat away the trees,
Age takes the tissues of a man and at last his name.

A *Major Work*

Poems are hard to read
Pictures are hard to see
Music is hard to hear
And people are hard to love

But whether from brute need
Or divine energy
At last mind eye and ear
And the great sloth heart will move.

THE PURPOSE of these few notes is to supply the reader with information that seems relevant but not integral to some of the poems. Notes of this sort are liable to affront a certain kind of reader, often the sort a poet values most. (Mr. Dudley Fitts, for instance, found the notes in my last book 'appallingly silly'). But I feel they are valid in alleviating one quite unnecessary kind of obscurity, the kind that arises from mere lack of special information.

MOST POETS live uneasily with Mr. Eliot's dire pronouncement: 'The most bungling form of obscurity is that of the poet who has not been able to express himself *to* himself; the shoddiest form is found when the poet is trying to persuade himself that he has something to say when he hasn't.' John Ciardi has offered a definition more comfortable to the poet but much harder to believe about one's own poems: 'Obscurity is what happens when a writer undertakes a theme and method for which the reader is not sufficiently prepared.' Clearly notes are powerless to correct difficulties as grave as the ones Mr. Eliot or Mr. Ciardi describe.

NOTRE DAME DE CHARTRES: *The Gothic cathedral which was built at Chartres in the 12th century was destroyed, together with most of the town, by a great fire in 1194. The survival of the Sacred Tunic of the Virgin, a gift of Charles the Bald in 876 and one of the chief relics of Christendom, inspired the building of the present basilica. Guillaume le Breton, historian and court poet to Philip Augustus, wrote: "At this time the Virgin and Mother of God, who is called and indeed shown to be the Lady of Chartres, wanted the sanctuary that is so specially hers to be more worthy of her. She therefore permitted the old and inadequate church to become the victim of flames, thus making room for the present basilica, which has no equal throughout the entire world." (Quoted by Otto von Simson in* The Gothic Cathedral, *New York, 1956).*

FROM RITUAL TO ROMANCE: *Through T. S. Eliot's poem* The Wasteland, *Jessie L. Weston's study of the Grail legend, from which this poem borrows its title, has supplied some of the principal images of modern poetry. It is primarily Mr. Eliot's version of the myth of the Fisher King that is invoked here.*

A VIEW OF THE BROOKLYN BRIDGE (lines 4–5): *The Brooklyn Bridge was designed by J. A. Roebling who began the work in 1869 which his son W. A. Roebling completed in 1883.*

AN ACCOUNT OF A VISIT TO HAWAII (line 24): *The New Year is the occasion for elaborate fireworks in the Hawaiian Islands (as in the Orient) and their extensive use throughout the year suggests that they are a compensation for the absence of blizzards, daffodils, pumpkins, etc. for seasonal demarcations.*

Stanza 6 ". . . . in 1809, two brothers, the American ship Captains Jonathan Winship of the 'Albatross' and Nathan Winship of the 'O'Cain', started on a voyage that established the sandlewood trade. After trading for furs on the coast of Oregon, they sailed in October, 1811, for Honolulu, where they and Captain William Heath Davis of the 'Isabella' took on cargoes of sandlewood. The ships sailed to Canton, where the fragrant wood was sold at a large profit. Returning to Honolulu, the three captains persuaded King Kamehameha I to grant them a monopoly of the sandlewood and cotton trade for ten years. Loading five ships, the three captains sailed to Canton and thus established a highly remunerative traffic. . . . the sandlewood trade developed rapidly and throve from 1815 to 1826. The successive Hawaiian kings at first followed the example of the shrewd Kamehameha I and kept sandlewood as a royal monopoly, but later they shared it with the higher chiefs. Taxes, to be paid in sandlewood, were levied on the district chiefs, who in turn levied them on their retainers, the people. Wanting some of the white man's ships, the king bought several, paying for them, it is said, with an equal or double tonnage of sandlewood. For measuring the amount, a rectangular pit the size of the greatest length, breadth and depth of the hull was dug, then filled with sandlewood logs. These pits are still reported in various parts of the islands and there is one, identified by the late Albert F. Judd, at about 800 feet elevation on the Kapalama-Nuuanu ridge on the grounds of the Kamehameha School, Honolulu.

"After the death of Kamehameha I in 1819, his successor ruled, but without the sagacity and shrewdness of the great king. Their sandlewood monopoly still seemed to them an inexhaustible source of wealth. . . . They bought so recklessly that the national debt (or royal debt) amounted to $300,000 by 1824. . . . Tax levies were increased until they became an intolerable burden on the people; at the same time the wood being gathered was smaller and of poor quality. After 1825-26 the trade declined steadily; by 1820–31 the trade was virtually finished." (Harold St. John in Pacific Science, vol. 1, no. 1, January 1947, pp. 5–20).

TO ABSENT FRIENDS (line 2): *Two limericks, by Ronald Arbuthnot Knox and a champion of Bishop Berkeley, explore this Idealist position more searchingly than the present poem does.*

> There once was a man who said: 'God
> Must think it exceedingly odd
> That the sycamore tree
> Continues to be
> When there's no one about in the quad.'

> Dear Sir:
> Your astonishment's odd.
> I am always about in the quad,
> And that's why the tree
> Will continue to be
> Since observed by yours faithfully,
> God.

TWO JAPANESE POEMS: *'Picture of a Castle'   A daimyo was a feudal Japanese overlord.*

'At the Kabuki-za'   The Kabuki-za is the home of the Kabuki theater in Tokyo. Performers make important entrances and exits on a ramp running through the audience to the back of the theater. This ramp is called the hanamichi *or* flowerway, *although as Earle*

Ernst points out in his excellent book The Kabuki Theatre (*New York, 1956*) *the compound is so familiar in this usage that the Japanese probably do not hear the metaphor any longer. The repertory of the Kabuki, and many of its traditions, are closely tied up with the* joruri *or puppet theater, and many of the gestures of the puppets are conventionalized by the actors.*

THREE OCCASIONAL POEMS: '*A Christmas Rune*' *Two archaic words here,* frore *meaning* frozen (*and modifying* 'time of year' *understood*) *and* foison *meaning* rich harvest, *are used principally to achieve the effect of an Anglo-Saxon charm or rune, the effect, that is, of a deliberate puzzle.*

RUS IN URBE (lines 2–3): *These two images are first, the Hindu god represented with many arms radiating from his shoulders and second, the genealogy of Christ depicted, as frequently in medieval art, in the form of a tree with human flowers.*

TREES IN A GROVE (line 18): *Gerard Manley Hopkins' sonnet on Duns Scotus' Oxford (which opens 'Towery city and branchy between towers') is quoted in line 14. Matthew Arnold's graceful note on Joseph Glanvil's* Vanity of Dogmatizing *is so integral a part of 'The Scholar-Gipsy' that one is always astonished at anthologists like Quiller-Couch who omit it.*

THE INVENTORS (lines 29–30): *Amerigo Vespucci, born in Florence in 1451 and early employed as a clerk in the enterprises of the Medici, had removed to Seville by 1492. When the king of Spain cancelled the monopoly granted to Columbus, Vespucci, then a ship-fitter, claims to have sailed on one of the first "free-lance" expeditions from Cadiz in May 10, 1497, and to have reached the American mainland on June 16th, or 8 days earlier than John Cabot. The early and uncontradicted claims that Vespucci advanced in letters to Italy resulted in the naming of the new world after him, although it is unlikely that he was even a member of the 1497 expedition.*

WILLIAM MEREDITH was born in New York City in 1919, went to secondary schools in Connecticut and Massachusetts, and was graduated from Princeton University. From 1941 to 1946 he was in military service, for the last four years as a naval aviator. *Love Letter from an Impossible Land*, his first volume of poems, appeared in the Yale Series of Younger Poets in 1944, with an introduction by Archibald MacLeish.

In 1946 he returned to Princeton where he was successively an instructor of English, a Woodrow Wilson Fellow, and Resident Fellow in Creative Writing, in which capacity he was assistant to R. P. Blackmur. His second book of poems, *Ships and Other Figures*, appeared in 1948.

He has received three prizes from Poetry Magazine and in 1956 he was awarded the Hudson Review Fellowship in Poetry. In recent years he has taught at the University of Hawaii, served two years of active naval duty during the Korean War, and taught creative writing at Connecticut College, where he is presently an assistant professor of English.

The first edition of THE OPEN SEA AND OTHER POEMS *consists of* 1000 COPIES *printed from type. The book was composed and printed by* CLARKE & WAY *at* THE THISTLE PRESS, *New York; bound by* H. WOLFF, *New York; paper manufactured by* S. D. WARREN COMPANY, *Boston; designed by* HARRY FORD.

THE TEXT *of the book was set on the Monotype in a typeface called* WALBAUM, *cut early in the nineteenth century by J. E. Walbaum, a type founder at Goslar and Weimar, who followed Didot in the design of this modern face. His original matrices are still in existence, and are the property of the Berthold foundry, of Berlin, Germany.*

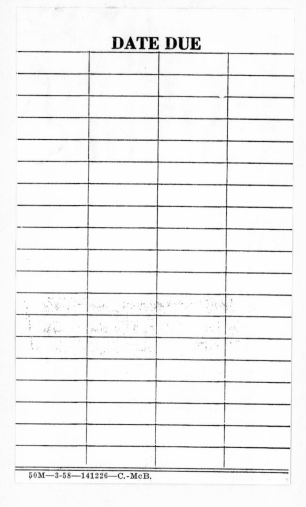

DATE DUE